DR.CHITRA REDDY

RE BOOT. INVENT. CHARGE.

HOW TO UP YOUR GAME AND FIND YOUR BLISS!

BEEJA
HOUSE

ISBN : 978-93-93635-23-5 (Paperback)

Published by: Beeja House

First Printing Edition 2022
Author Email: chitrareddy66@gmail.com

www.drchitrareddy.com

Dedication

This book is dedicated to my mother,

Dr Leela Bai, an amazing clinician, a dedicated doctor, an exemplary wife, mother and grandmother, but most of all, an outstanding human being, my muse and my hero.

Contents

Foreword

"Happiness is a state of mind" and "Happiness comes from within" are oft repeated, clichéd responses we get from friends and counsellors alike when we approach them with life's predicaments, more often created by our own vacillating mental health from time to time. The most common ' situation ' happens to be that 'midlife' crisis many of us go through in our personal, professional and social lives. How do such situations arise and what are the basic steps one can proactively take to lead a fulfilled life has been very lucidly enunciated by Dr. Chitra Reddy in this book, "Reboot. Reinvent. Recharge".

Happiness can be found even in the darkest times if one only remembers to switch on the light is J.K. Rowling's convincing quote through her fictional character Dumbledore. Dr. Chitra's book is the right recipe for this metaphorical light to be permanently switched on throughout our lives.

I have known Dr. Chitra for over three decades; all through these years, I have observed how she has been and remained a huge positive influence on whoever she comes in contact with. Dr. Chitra's positivity and enthusiasm always rubs off on those around her creating that experience of "Hygge" (Norwegian for well-being) in her immediate environment. While I have never seriously attempted to analyse the source of this perennial positivity in her, I guess it has its roots in the number of lives she has brought into this world as a medical practitioner of great repute and the immense fulfilment this professional experience has given to her heart and soul. Endowed with such an exceptional and inspiring attitude for life, she has combined her natural flair for writing with all her mundane experiences over the years to create this exquisite panacea for ensuring a fulfilled life. Having put most of these tenets into practice and having experienced them in her own life, I am convinced all that Dr. Chitra offers to the readers in this book is practical, realistic and achievable and not just theory.

What is impressive about this book is that the eight pillars of Happiness viz. Perspective, Humility, Humour, Acceptance, Forgiveness, Gratitude, Compassion and Generosity have all been vividly illustrated through the author's own day to day experiences that readers from all walks of life can relate to. The absence of jargon and more importantly verbose philosophy, which is not uncommon in themes like this, has made this book easy to read, simple to understand and worthwhile to act upon.

Last, but certainly not the least, all of us need to internalise sooner than later that life is not just about knowing how to survive the storm but also learning how to dance in the rain. 'Reboot. Reinvent. Recharge' provides us this know-how by emphasising that the raison d'etre of life is long lasting happiness leading to soulful fulfilment. I am delighted to share with the readers that my key takeaway from this book is this simple equation:

Reboot + Reinvent + Recharge = Rejuvenation.

I do hope that your takeaway would be this too.

G.S. Sundararajan
Financial Services Consultant
Ex MD, SME
Citibank, India.

Acknowledgements

This book has been a spiritual journey and I have learnt as much writing it as I hope my readers will learn from reading it. It has made me rethink, reboot, reinvent and recharge and I would like to thank each one of you for picking up this book and reading it.

It has made me a better person and compelled me to follow every bit of advice therein. I hope it will make you grow as an individual and enable you to be the best version of yourself.

I will always be grateful to my mother, Dr. Leela Bai, for inspiring me and imparting her quest for answers, her curiosity about anything and everything, her knowledge, her wisdom, her deep sense of self and her love of humanity.

I would especially like to thank my husband Ravi and my daughter Yashica for always encouraging me to do whatever makes me happy and for all their inputs.

I would like to thank my dearest friends Anita, Prathima, Yamuna and Usha for being my sounding boards and all my other dear friends (too many to name) for all their support and encouragement.

I am extremely grateful to G.S. Sundararajan for so kindly agreeing to write the foreword at such short notice and doing a rocking job.

I am truly thankful to Saakshi Kaushal, my coordinator for her patience with someone who is rather tech-challenged and without whom this book would not have seen the light of day.

Last, but not least, I am immensely thankful to Geetika Saigal, my mentor and coach for giving me the courage to get this book off the ground and see it through.

Introduction

Have you been feeling a little slow lately? A bit like your laptop with too many programs running? Like your laptop, do you feel like you need virus protection? Not the COVID vaccine kind. Just something to buffer you from the ups and downs of life? Do you get the feeling life's a bit like a treadmill… where you're constantly running and yet find yourself in the same place?

Are you wondering why in spite of all your achievements, wealth and success, you find a certain '*je ne sais quoi*' missing? If you're wondering why you're not feeling fulfilled, happy or content, this book is for you. I don't have answers to the why, but I have definitely tried to answer the how… how you can change your perspective, how to **REBOOT, REINVENT AND RECHARGE.**

It is not a treatise on philosophy, it is a simple guide that will show you a direction, much like the runway lights that direct a plane to land. You are the pilot and you will have to navigate your way to a safe landing right up to the parking bay.

We all know what to do when the situation is someone else's, but when it comes to our own lives, we're often too close to the picture and need a gentle push in the right direction. Sometimes we need to hear it from someone else.

I have found that though tons of people find success and transit at temples and places of worship either before or after their success, few understand spirituality or the concept of finding happiness within. I hope this book will make you introspect, reflect and rethink.

I wish you contentment.

Dr Chitra Reddy.

Chapter 1

Assessing Your Life - A Balance Sheet

"All my life, I wanted to be somebody. Now I see that I should have been more specific.
"If your dreams don't scare you, they're too small."

Richard Branson

Several years ago, while on a flight to Mexico, I happened to make the acquaintance of a businessman who owned a winery in France. During our conversation, he parted with some wonderful advice.

"Almost all of us make business our life," he said. "What we forget to do is make life our business. At the end of each year, we spend days chalking up our assets and our liabilities, our profits, expenses and losses, our investments, stocks and shares until we have everything neatly balanced. We begin another year by planning our goals for the future, our short and long-term investments and how much money we'd like to make. We have a fairly clear idea of where we stand. But why don't we do that with our lives?"

I pondered on this question, the rest of the way and I figured he had a lot of truth in those words. We often spend days agonising over small decisions like whether to spend two thousand rupees on that gorgeous dress or ten thousand on that leather briefcase, but we invest very little thought on something as major as our lives!

We function on auto pilot, getting up, getting ready, getting to work, and getting back until yet another day has passed us by.

A business that appears to be doing pretty well, with a reasonably good turnover, maybe only just breaking even or possibly even going under with the weight of overheads and unnecessary expenses. Only a balance sheet will give you the correct picture. So it is with life!

Regardless of whether or not you are happy with the way your life is going, take valuable time off to make an honest assessment. You lose nothing and stand to gain a lot. But don't do it under pressure or in a hurry. Like a balance sheet, even a small miscalculation could make you see red.

Find a quiet, peaceful corner when you have at least an hour to contemplate. It could be at home or on a bus or train journey or even when you're going on a long drive. Close your eyes (obviously not when you're driving) and think calmly. If you're going through a bad patch, try and focus your mind away from the current problem. It could distort your overall image. Go back to the beginning, even your childhood if you like. But the best part is that you can begin wherever it suits you, as long as you integrate the major pieces of your life. Now that you have a recap of past and current events, get down to brass tacks, the task of actually assessing your life and doing something about it.

STEP 1

WRITE DOWN YOUR GOALS IN TWO DISTINCT COLUMNS

SHORT TERM	LONG TERM

What you envisage as short or long-term is entirely up to you. It is highly individualistic and circumstantial. For example, to a twenty-year-old, a long-term goal may be achieving XYZ things by the age of forty, possibly forging ahead in a tough career, finding a significant other, having a kid or two, or a house with a picket fence and maybe a dog.

To a seventy-year-old, it may mean something as simple as visiting a grandchild in another town or country within the year.

Goals are not necessarily humongous, near impossible or lead-weighted. That's not to say one can't dream big. But they may be as simple as planting a rose bush or weeding the garden. Goals are only another way of anchoring your thoughts and channelizing your energies in the right direction.

To guide you, I have listed some common short-term and long-term goals.

SHORT TERM GOALS

- To lose at least 5 kilos in 3 months.
- To start going on that morning walk tomorrow.
- To buy mom a gift.
- To send off that "Thank you" card today.
- To join that computer class this month.
- To sew those buttons today.
- To stop losing your temper unnecessarily.
- To make up your mind and get that new haircut tomorrow.
- To take a doctor's appointment now.
- To call Meena and get that fabulous cake recipe
- To call the Sharma's for dinner over the weekend.
- To apply for that bank loan for your house, business or car.

- To make that project report for the business you intend to start, by this weekend.

As you might have noticed, the above list has a lot of things that people think of doing, but somehow never get around to doing. The simple act of putting it down on paper, let's us see how trivial or how important they are and actually goads us into action – possibly something as simple as picking up the phone and making a call that will set things in motion.

For example, once you have actually picked up the phone and invited the Sharmas for dinner on Saturday, you have no choice but to start planning the menu, buying the groceries, tidying up the house and actually doing it with enthusiasm.

Of course, if you are the type who hates entertaining at home, you will end up taking them out for dinner, but you would have at least got it over with or actually ended up having a good time. If your dinner at home goes off well, then you're left with a feeling of contentment. So would an evening out without the additional chores of cooking and cleaning. In the unfortunate event that the evening was a disaster by way of food or company, look at it this way – at least it's over and done with! Now what's having dinner with some friends got to do with my happiness, you ask. I'm getting there, believe me.

Happiness is all about positive reinforcement, which in turn increases the level of your endorphins, the happy hormones. They are nothing but minute quantities of chemicals released in the brain in certain situations, resulting in a happy feeling.

So, what do we need to do to increase those levels? We manoeuvre ourselves into situations that give us a sense of achievement, pride, contentment etc. Even if it is something as small as paying your colleague a compliment and watching her beam. Her smile says to you, "That was really sweet of you" or "You have good taste" or "I like you for saying that."

This in turn gives your happy hormones a boost, thus making you feel good. And happiness is nothing but feeling good. In essence, you have made yourself happy. How easy was that?

It is for that very reason that something as simple as starting off on that morning walk or getting a new hairstyle can give that extra pep and that added spring in your step. You're unconsciously telling the world, "Look at me! I finally managed to get into my fitness routine. I exercise. Do you?" Or "Look at my new haircut! Don't I look great?

It gives your self-confidence a boost, in turn giving you that special inner glow that turns heads. Maybe that's what beauty queens mean when they talk about inner beauty! That, in turn, reinforces your self-esteem, sending your endorphins into a tizzy. It often explains why people who changed something about themselves, be it looks, style of dressing or career often look better and more confident. We often tend to accept unequivocally that quality that someone is projecting rather than the quality itself.

This reminds me of the boys in my class at medical school way back when. In the days preceding any test or exam, most of us girls went around looking tense and studious, our minds preoccupied with how to get the better of those microorganisms that seemed to cause a zillion diseases and were determined to make life miserable for us poor mortals who had to master what they did when, how, where and why!

The boys, on the other hand, went around looking blissfully happy, much like the subjects of our study, with not a care in the world.

Come the day of the exam, they would lounge around outside the exam hall chewing gum while we chewed our nails down to the pulps of our fingers. Finally, one of them would casually ask, "By the way, did you girls read up on so and so"?" referring to some vague, little-known disease, symptom or organism that he had dredged up from some little-known book or footnote. It would immediately send us into panic mode. Whereupon, we would all grab our books, desperately turning pages trying to find the obscure little so and so, to no avail

Ask any girl how she's done her exams and she'll likely say, "Okay" or "Went well." Ask any boy and he'll say, "It was a breeze!" or "Cool!" or "I maxed the paper!" Come results and we would wait anxiously for our turns to peer at the notice board. Those were the days before mobiles and online results. Invariably, the maxers always fell short of their expectations and well short of our own marks. What I'm trying to say here is not that you shouldn't feel confident. On the contrary, I'm telling you exactly the opposite. No matter how hard we had studied or how sure we were to do well, we let someone else's confidence undermine us. We went strictly by what the boys were PROJECTING! Whether or not they were thorough, they PROJECTED a complete and thorough knowledge of their subject.

So what does it achieve, you may well ask. Life, my friend, is full of situations where the person you PROJECT is more important than the person you are.

Hang on! I don't want to be an impostor, you scream! Or maybe just mumble! I don't want to project something I am not, you cry indignantly. I laud your integrity, your innate sincerity. And so my friend, I suggest we compromise. Why not aim at becoming what you want to project?

This is where we come to **LONG TERM GOALS.**

My eighth-grade teacher once asked us what each of us wanted to be when we grew up. In our class of twenty-two, almost ten hands went up in favour of becoming doctors and mine was one of them.

"Who wants to be a writer?" she asked the class. Two and a half hands went up. Mine was the half, but it soon came down. My mother is a well-known gynaecologist. I had always imagined myself as a doctor because I simply loved what she did.

But right since I was in eighth grade, I had this dream of writing a novel and becoming famous, not as a doctor, but as an author. Throughout the rest of school and medical school, I wrote a few articles, some poems and some amazing letters that my friends enjoyed reading in times when snail mail ruled. My passion for writing was always at the back of my mind.

It is simply amazing how pleasurable it is to pursue your goals, regardless of the final result. Ask any professional hockey or football player who mucked up all the penalty shots in his last match, if he ever thought of quitting the game and he'll look at you as if you'd lost your marbles.

What I'm arriving at is that when you have long-term goals that you actually care about or are passionate about, you not only have a much better chance of achieving them, but you will also enjoy the journey. Of course, with the added benefit of elevating your endorphins.

I'm aware that Napoleon Bonaparte claimed that the word "impossible" didn't exist. But for lesser mortals like me, the word crops up at fairly regular intervals. For example, things that would figure on my list of impossible things would go something like this:

- Standing on my head for thirty seconds
- Climbing Mount Everest
- Hitting the gym on a regular basis
- Listening to more than one Zoom meeting in a day
- Visiting more than one relative a week

The list is endless. The point I'm trying to make here is that not everyone is capable of doing everything that someone else can do, nor is it necessary to do so.

Therefore, **CHOOSE YOUR GOALS CAREFULLY.**

Think of your life as a set of building blocks. You can build only those structures that can possibly be assembled with the blocks in your possession. Your neighbour might have built a truck, but only because he has the requisite blocks and wheels in hand. What you can do is work towards acquiring a new set of blocks that enable you to make that ten-ton truck. Don't even dream of stealing those blocks! Life is a series of small goals and at every step, we can work towards acquiring newer and better building blocks that can up the game.

To start with, list out your **LONG TERM GOALS.** As before, I'll help you get going by giving a few examples.

LONG TERM GOALS

- To start an advertising agency.
- To do that B.Ed degree or Montessori training.
- To open a play school.
- To qualify as a doctor, engineer, or lawyer.
- To build a house of your own or buy your own home.
- To write a book.
- To master certain skills like baking, sewing etc.
- To upskill.
- To learn to play a musical instrument.

As you can see, none of the above things can be achieved or acquired in a day. They require years of effort and single-mindedness. This is precisely why one has to want them badly enough.

The basic tenet of achieving something is:

TO WANT IT BADLY ENOUGH.

It's a start, but that in itself is not going to make things happen, as you well know. If you have really made up your mind about what you want, **GO FOR IT.**

I know any number of people who think they want something, then give up halfway if the going gets

slightly tough. Then, regret it for the rest of their lives. It may even be the girl you want. Why? Because they think they're **NOT GOOD ENOUGH.** But you will never know unless you try.

Remember to **have faith in yourself.** It can truly work wonders. Ask any author who has received a dozen rejection slips from publishers what really kept them going, and they will tell you, it was nothing but faith in their work and themselves. If not, no self-reliant person would even think of sending their material to yet another publisher.

Dick King-Smith, an Englishman and author of the book, "The Sheep-Pig," which was made into the box office hit," Babe," wrote his first book at the age of fifty-six. Since then, he has churned out 90 books from the same small room where his first book saw the light of day. By 76, he was publishing a new book every three or four months, notwithstanding the fact that he lacked a college education and had eleven grandchildren, who I'm sure kept him busy. As a farmer who lived with animals all his life, he tells it like it is. And that's because he knew what he was talking about. Like King-Smith, it takes some people almost all their lives to figure out what they really want to do. And it's important to remember that

SUCCESS DOES NOT COME EARLY TO EVERYONE.

Not everyone is destined to be a Jeff Bezos or a J.K. Rowling. One can never cross the river by walking halfway on the bridge.

AND IT WILL NEVER HAPPEN AT ALL IF YOU GIVE UP HALFWAY. PERSEVERE.

ASSESSING YOUR LIFE

Chapter 2
Thinking Positively - An Acquired Art

"The positive thinker sees the invisible, feels the intangible and achieves the impossible."

Winston Churchill

Fortunately for me, I'm a born optimist. Not everyone is so lucky. At any given time, for every optimist born, there must be at least two who enter this world groaning. The optimist is born crying too, the only difference being, that he does it with gusto, bringing a smile to his Obstetrician's face.

But take heart! Don't believe everyone who tells you that a pessimist is an experienced optimist. Experience could never put an optimist down.

Let me tell you a little secret. First, learn to build castles. In the air, I mean. Nothing on earth, no amount of riches, honours, not even a real castle in the heart of Scotland could give you as much pleasure as the ones you build, brick by brick, in your own head. It is the truly magical, extremely potent power of your imagination that can transform your life permanently and forever. Even if you live in a dingy, one-room studio. It can make you a princess, transport you to exotic locations, dress you to the nines, bathe you in perfume and intoxicate you with champagne. Dom Perignon, no less! **ABSOLUTELY FREE!** All you have to do is learn to enjoy it!

The day I passed my MD in Gynaecology, I sat at my table, imagining myself getting hassled by the queue of patients waiting to see me, how busy and how important I would be, and how the word would get around about my clinical acumen and my surgical prowess. The reality turned out to be a whole lot different. It took years of hard work to establish a practice, a name and a loyal clientele. But I truly enjoyed the experience of those few moments when I had transported myself to a place where I wanted to be. So much so that I still remember it vividly. It had cost me nothing, harmed no one and afforded immense pleasure, besides boosting my ego and my morale. I came away with the feeling that at some point in life, I had something to look forward to. This particular feeling is very important, in that it gives you a sense of purpose, a destination that makes your journey worthwhile. Never mind the delays, the flat tyres or faulty detours. One knows where one is actually headed, and that makes all the hurdles seem like minor irritants.

Picture the other side of the coin. Here I am, sitting at my table, having just learnt that I've got through my MD exam. I'm happy, my friends walk in and congratulate me. I realise that they're also from my town and are going to be practising nearby. I start wondering how on earth I'm going to compete with three other Gynaecologists practising in the same neighbourhood. What if my practice doesn't take off at all? What if I don't get a job? How am I going to invest so much in a clinic? What if I decide to start one a little away from the town centre? How will I commute? What about my fuel bills? Whoa! Hold it right there! You are surely heading in the right direction if your destination is depression. Now, I'm not asking you to abandon logic and practicality in favour of dreams. Not at all.

All I ask is that you enjoy your success, at least for a while. Then sit down to practicalities, work around your problems and come up with solutions to tackle them. Try this line of thought –

Gosh! So now I have another three Gynecs practically next door. What can I do to fare better? Clubbing them over their heads and hiding their bodies is definitely out of the question. All the more for a doc. How about if I did an additional course, something that would give me an advantage and make me stand out? A special course in infertility or laparoscopy. How about a weekend practice in the suburbs? Anyway, I'll work on the logistics and come up with something. But for now, it's time to get ready to **PARTY!**

Admittedly, for someone who doesn't think along those lines in the natural course, it would take years of practice, but even if you consciously try a new line of thinking, you're winning. Why? Because you have actually committed to yourself that other possibilities exist, you have thrown away those blinds and are finally looking at life through a wide-angle lens – in **TECHNICOLOUR!**

Nothing in life is all bad and no person on earth is all bad either. It probably sounds naive, but very few people in this world actually take the trouble to dig beneath the surface and find out the truth. When we hear about someone's faults or misfortunes, we lap it up with enthusiasm, always game for more juicy tidbits. How often do we even bother to clarify the facts or give it the benefit of doubt before we come to our own conclusions? We have no doubts that we're hearing the truth.

By the same token, let someone tell us that her new neighbour brought across a pound of homemade cake and we'll ask, "Oh my! How sweet! But what does she want from you?"

"Why don't we take that at face value too?"

Tell a patient that she is not likely to have put on 6 kilos in the last 3 months on account of her contraceptive pills and she will not believe you. Telling her that thousands of papers have been published on the effects of OC pills on weight gain and that she will definitely not get cancer, will not convince her. Tell her that you delivered a baby with two heads and she will be very ready to take your word for it. What are the odds of that happening?" I ask

People are always ready to believe the worst of anybody and anything, but they take forever to believe anything good about anyone or anything. And end up wasting years of their lives in self-doubt and in doubting others.

I once spent about $54 playing the German NFL lottery. I'm not by nature the gambling type and I never buy a lottery ticket, even if it were to be Rs.10 or the equivalent of one penny. But one fine day, I received this form in the post and was tempted to turn into a millionaire overnight. Having to remit the requisite amount in US dollars, I was forced to make two trips to the bank to collect a demand draft for the said amount. This was before the days when GPay and credit cards were in common usage in India. Two months after posting the self-addressed stamped envelope, I had heard nothing from them. But I didn't worry because I knew only one of two things could have happened. Either it was lost in transit, in which case my money was gone without the chance to play the lottery. Or they had taken my money and had no intention of sending me the ticket. I highly doubted the latter for two reasons. One, it was German. And two, it was Government-run. Then one fine day it arrived. Returned for insufficient postage. Apparently, the self-addressed stamped envelope was only meant for postage within Europe. I could have kicked myself. But my Demand draft was safe inside. I resent it with adequate postage. This time my ticket arrived within a week. But I waited endlessly for the 2 million Deutsche

Marks and Mercedes-Benz in vain. No harm hoping right?

Now, if you think this chapter is dedicated to encouraging everyone to download all their savings into little-known lotteries or unpredictable horses, think again. I don't encourage it at all. I'm all for saving. But I do believe that every once in a while one should give in to those impulses that tell us, "Do this! It's going to make you feel good."

It could be something as simple as taking an hour out to have coffee with a good friend, buying that wicked little dress/ lingerie/ stilettos, those groovy sunglasses or spending an extra half hour in bed or at the spa. What has this got to do with thinking positively, you ask? It has to do with believing that you deserve it. It's a positive reaffirmation of your self-worth. The reason we often neglect ourselves and our desires are because we most often think we don't deserve it. Or that we're not worth it. I would rather buy my little one shoes than splurge on that haircut. Or you may think "I already have so many dresses anyway." Good for you. But you can still bargain with yourself. Settle for the smart handbag you always wanted for Rs. 2000/ instead of the dress that would put you back by Rs. 3000/. You not only feel smart toting the bag, you feel smart for having saved yourself Rs. 1000/. In addition, you have subconsciously reaffirmed to yourself that you deserve it.

Do you want to save all of it and still feel good? It's possible. Just tell yourself that it was so smart of you not to give in to temptation. Now you can save for that dream holiday. Always have a target to look forward to. As you can see, you are slowly acquiring the delicate art of talking yourself into happiness, no matter what you decide to do or not do. Whether you splurge on a dress or save your money, you're still a winner- you're either worth the dress and look like a million bucks, or you're too smart to waste money and feel like a million bucks. Either way, you come out looking like an Archangel. Now, this is an attitude that needs cultivation in a hothouse – careful nurturing, warmth and watering. It could take years to grow, or die overnight. It could choke with the weeds around it, or it could encourage others to cultivate it. It took yours truly years, I might add. Think of it as an investment with lifelong returns, something like a coconut tree, but one that grows in a greenhouse.

Test this attitude out, right today. Apply it to any given situation and find out how you can come out of it smelling like a rose. Let me give you an example:

You've just come home and your son/ daughter/ husband is in the living room watching TV. You realise it's time for your favourite program to come on. You grab the remote and change channels. It's followed by loud wails of protest there are two options –

Option one - give in and let them watch. You may even end up liking it if you actually sit down to it.

Option two – you can decide if it's actually fair to be deprived of the one program that you actually get to watch the whole day. If you think not, you can suggest they can watch a rerun of their channel and watch this with you. They/ he/ she might actually end up liking it. That's the upside. The downside is that certain doors may be banged shut a little too loudly for comfort. No matter! They'll come around. But are you miserable? Don't be!

If you're asking me "What for?" then you're heading in the right direction. If you're miserable because you missed the program, then think of yourself as a noble, self-sacrificing goat, but stop bleating for heaven's sake. If you're miserable because you upset someone, think of it as their well-deserved lesson in the art of pleasing others for a change. Pat yourself on the back for finally being able to put yourself first and put your foot down. You deserve it as much as the next person. If your family crawls back to the living room and quietly settles down on the couch, consider it as a bonus. MISERABLE? How on earth do you spell that?

Now that you have learnt the art of being persistently upbeat and hopeful, let me remind you that it has its consequences. You could be so hopeful about everything you undertake that there is the risk of being absolutely and utterly disappointed when things don't really pan out the way you hoped they would. And that could send you into the mother of all depressions if you're not prepared. So what's the use, you ask. Better to be pessimistic and prepare for the worst, rather than hope for the best and end up with the worst.

There is a subtle difference, *mon ami*, but a difference nonetheless. With the former route, you're miserable from the start, whereas, with the latter path, you stand to be upset only if and when things are not going according to plan. To minimise this eventuality, I suggest you develop the art of planning ahead instead of worrying ahead! Refer to Chapter 1.

You've worked hard, have done your best and are hoping desperately to get into electronics/ medicine/ architecture/ law. In the event that you don't get a place, your misery gets diluted if you already have a game plan.

For example, I had an inkling I may not make it to medicine. I had decided that I'd opt for my second choice, namely, journalism/ architecture. Who knows, I may end up being a better architect than I would have ever been as a doctor. So I listed out the advantages of my second choice over the first –

- Shorter course
- Shorter working hours
- No 24-36 hour duties
- No duties ever for the rest of your life

- Cannot leave knife/ swab/ scissors in anyone's insides (just kidding)
- Will have more time for family and friends
- Will be able to get sozzled on the weekend without wondering when your hospital might call
- Will be able to take off on long weekends at short notice
- Will be able to pursue other interests- eg. travelling, cooking, gardening, music or painting. Can delegate my workload unlike in private practice.
- You're not responsible for the mismanagement of your patients by your colleagues while you're away.
- Need not work on Sundays, holidays, festivals or at odd hours.
- Need not pass endless exams till you're 50 in order to keep upto date or upgrade your knowledge.
- Need not keep investing in newer and more expensive equipment like laparoscopes or ultrasound machines.
- May actually earn more than a doctor.
- The list is endless.
- Alternatively, let us assume that you did not get into electronics/ architecture but ended up doing medicine, always assuming that you have a basic interest/ aptitude for the subject.
- Look at the plus side:

- It's a respectable, noble profession.
- It requires hard work and long hours, but none of it is wasted.
- It gives a sense of achievement on completion.
- It gives a sense of fulfilment like no other.
- The ability to save lives is unparalleled.
- You can relieve hundreds of people from pain and suffering.
- You can counsel and make a difference in people's lives.
- You will know enough medical specialists should you require any treatment for yourself or your family.
- You belong to an elite class of people, one that carries its own awe.
- Anything else you do other than your profession is doubly appreciated. For example, cooking, playing a game or an instrument.
- Can earn more than most professionals.

As you can see, for every situation in life, there is plenty to laud and plenty to crib about. The point is to decide which one of them you're going to spend most of your life doing.

Let's assume you have already jumped onto one bandwagon and realise too late it's the wrong one, quite apart from the fact that it's going at ninety miles per hour on its way to the circus. With no stops for coffee either.

Clearly, jumping off a moving wagon would cause you serious damage. You have two options – learn to play the banjo and learn it well. Or else, hang onto your seat and enjoy the view till you reach the circus and decide your act. If neither of these options excites you, I suggest you make time for your third and most productive activity while on the move, and learn to sing as well!

If I sound like I'm talking in riddles, forgive me. All I'm trying to say is that once you've married your vocation, either stick to it for better or for worse, for richer or poorer (hopefully temporary), in sickness and in health, till death do you part, while you figure out how to make time for your paramour or true love, be it writing, music, teaching, art, web designing or a cookery show on YouTube.

Else stick it out for a while, save some money, get divorced from your uninteresting job and make a clean break. Think of your experience in that particular field as alimony. Better still, think of it as an extra qualification. For example, once a doctor, always a doctor! That knowledge can never go to waste. Nor can anything that you've learnt at your previous job.

But one word of advice. Don't jump into anything new without a careful and complete study of what you intend to do. A known devil is always better than an unknown one.

Be positive about the choices you want to make. But that should be preceded by sufficient groundwork and research. If you've done your homework well, there's every reason to hope for success. But it's absolutely foolish to expect 90% in an exam without studying for it. Believe in yourself.

IT'S SURE TO MAKE YOU THINK POSITIVELY!

COUNT YOUR BLESSINGS

Chapter 3

Make Others Happy - It Rubs Off

"Money alone can't make you happy, but everyone wants to find out for themselves."

If one takes a few minutes to ponder on the things in life that give us the most pleasure, it would become patently obvious that for us to be happy, someone or something has to give something away. And more often than not, that someone has to be you.

The fragrance of a flower, the light from the sun, the smile of a child, the song of a bird, these are things that would be of no consequence unless dispensed. Can a flower appreciate its own fragrance, or the Sun its own light? Obviously not! But what a world of difference they make to their recipients!

Spreading happiness is akin to spreading sunshine – with one added benefit – it rubs off on you! As a teenager, I suffered from an obsessive-compulsive disorder, that of buying cards for anyone and everyone for any occasion whatsoever. Those were the days when virtual cards, Facebook and Instagram dint exist. Almost all my pocket money was spent on gifts and cards. Today, as an adult, a significant part of my earnings is still spent on gifts for close friends and relatives. I'm of course constantly wondering how I've ended up spending so much, but I would hate to do otherwise.

There is more to a gift than finishing an obligation. First of all, there is the planning and choosing. Of course, this applies only to close friends and family or people you really care about. Then comes the budgeting and shopping, the selection, the wrapping, the giving and last but certainly not the least, the joy on the other person's face. Admittedly, the moment may be fleeting, but it is enough to warm the cockles of your heart for a long time to come. Strangely enough, even the memory of that moment can recreate that sense of happiness and warmth.

One of the hallmarks of this basic emotion we call happiness is its fleeting nature. It can be induced by any one of the five senses, be it sight, smell, touch, taste or hearing. It takes no more than several split seconds for any of these stimuli to travel to the brain and activate those nerve endings to produce our "happy" hormones, more scientifically called serotonins. These sensations or the happy hormones themselves may not stay for long, but the memory of those sensations stays with us for long periods of time, sometimes even decades. And even if they have been forgotten, the memory of that happiness can be triggered by seeing a particular person or thing, hearing a particular voice or song, tasting a particular dish or something that reminds you of your mother's cooking, the smell of certain foods or the familiar touch of a loved one.

The current stimulus not only makes us happy, but also sets off a cascade of happy memories. A good example is a large family reunion. There's an abundance of familiar positive stimuli, a feast for all the sense organs, the sight of familiar people, the sound of familiar voices, the hugs, the smells of food that you've grown up on, and the smells of familiar people close to you (which may not be overtly obvious), and last but not the least, the taste of the food you love. Besides this, you will treasure the memory of that meeting for a long time to come.

Happiness is a peculiar commodity. The more you give, the more you get. However simple that sounds, it's also one of the most elusive things in the world, second only to money. It is as beautiful as a butterfly on wings, as transient as a rainbow and as elusive as a moonbeam. Yet, it is within reach of all of us, if only we could understand what we were actually looking for. One of medicine's best-known clichés is, "What the mind does not know, the eye does not see!"

Unfortunately, few of us in this world can actually recognise happiness when it is staring us in the face.

So first my friend, let us find out what we're actually looking for!

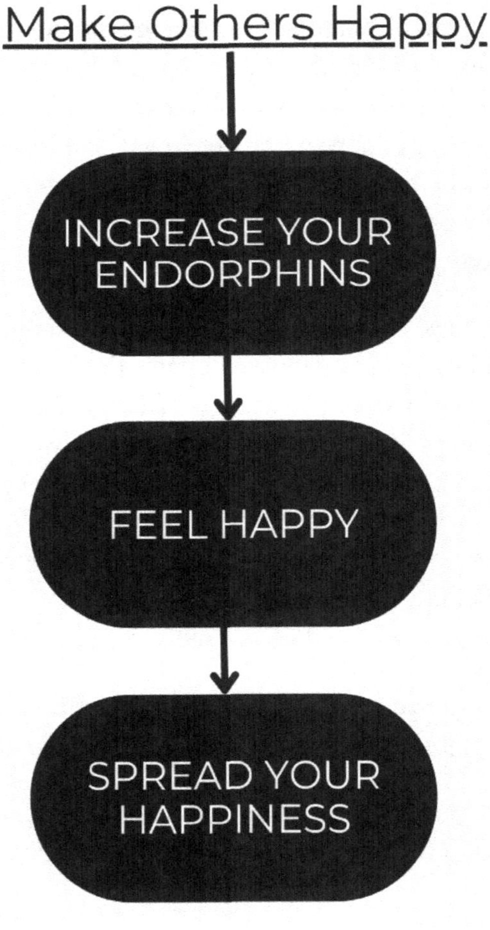
Make Others Happy
INCREASE YOUR ENDORPHINS
FEEL HAPPY
SPREAD YOUR HAPPINESS

Chapter 4

Count Your Blessings - You'll Be Surprised

"What you have taken for granted, someone is praying for."

When George Bernard Shaw said, "I cried because I had no shoes, then I saw a boy who had no feet"! He brought home in one sentence Man's totally inappropriate and misguided attitude to life – that of taking things for granted.

But man cannot be blamed, after all, among all the millions of species that God created on this earth, he's the only one with a mind of his own and the capacity to think. He has always been King of the jungle, or so he believes. And he can take things for granted.

The lion cannot take his food for granted, he has to chase his lunch, the camel cannot take his water for granted, he has to store it in his hump, the dolphin cannot take his air for granted, he has to swim up for air. But man can easily afford to, after all, he's capable of breathing his air at 35000 feet on a Jet plane or in his space station.

While the lion has no idea where his next meal is coming from, north or west, man has his lunch all chalked out, Indian, Chinese or Continental, and probably his dinner and breakfast as well. Good for him! Except, there's a minor detail - it makes him extremely complacent. Complacency, as you well know, is a fatal flaw. He could well be on the way to eating his way out of his resources pretty soon, or it could get him eaten up in a jungle. What I'm coming to, is not a long drawn-out lecture on ecological balance, but an appeal to open your eyes and see! If you ask me, I would say that a normal man is more visually challenged than a blind one. At least the blind man's other senses are in overdrive. But there's nothing more disheartening than a seeing man who will not see.

Ask anyone what could be better with his life and he will find a hundred things he could change, his job, his car, his mother-in-law, maybe even his wife! Ask him what's great about his life and he'll pause, dither, think hard and say something like, "I don't know if I can say great, but I do have an ok job and my kid's great!"(Provided she's not yet a teenager).

I'll bet 90% of men would never say my wife's great or vice versa. Why do you think so? After all, they married them right?

I'll tell you why... it's because they always expect more! When you marry the man of your dreams, you have already made plans for him, never mind any plans of his own. He's going to stop smoking, he's going to dote on me, give up his favourite chair in the bar, stop playing golf every weekend, take the kids to the park, stand next to me while I cook etc etc

When he marries the girl of his dreams, he's decided she'll be up bright and early with his steaming cup of coffee, cook delicious hot meals like his mama, let him play golf every free minute, have his boys night out and entice him with sinful lingerie every night!

The reality, my friend, is a long way off. He's probably never going to stop smoking (ask me), he may dote on you (when he can't find his shorts), of course, he won't give up his favourite chair at the bar and probably play golf at weekends and weekdays! Take the kids to the park? What park? Be happy if he doesn't say, what kids? Just kidding! But there are a few men who might be better off a few miles radius away from the kitchen.

About the girl of his dreams, well, he's welcome to dream – no tax on that! But bright and early may be cutting it too fine, on the other hand, she may be so bright and early that she's left to work before he can say, "Where are my pyjamas?" There go his hot meals along with the 7.05, as for it tasting like mama's cooking, it does! Her mama's, not his. Jeez, he'll take that, but what on earth has she got against his night out with the boys? Alright, maybe one or two girls as well. None of his doing, mind you. She's always chatting and gossiping with her girlfriends, so what about male bonding and all that stuff?

And Christ! Why doesn't she have a single piece of sexy black lingerie? She seriously doesn't expect him to buy it for her now, does she?

Welcome to the real world folks! In 70mm with Digital Dolby surround sound. What's wrong with expecting more, you ask? You're the one who expects us to dream, to believe that the sky's the limit. Then why I should settle for less, you demand! Right, I asked you to dream, but if I may refresh your memory, I asked you to dream, set a goal and go about turning it into reality. *Comprendez vous?*

Now let's be a little realistic here. Trying to turn every man into Bill Gates or Brad Pitt is not quite possible, even if he has the added qualification of being a school dropout. Nor is it easy to get him to quit smoking, golfing or turning him into a sous chef overnight.

The idea here is to focus on the pluses, not the minuses. Is he working his butt off trying to provide for you and the family and make life a little more than just comfortable? Is he an okay dad or even more than okay? Does he come home sozzled every night? Does he often let you do your own thing, be it meeting your friends and family, calling them over, buying your own clothes or home stuff? Does he refrain from hitting on other women? Does he have a good heart? Is he kind, generous and hardworking? Does he love you, though he doesn't say it in so many words?

Then you have hope, my girl. I'm not saying he's a candidate for the world's best husband or boyfriend, but I'm definitely saying hang on to what you have for dear life. And make it work. In fact, take out a book and write down all the things you hate and all the things you love about your man. You might actually surprise yourself. **DO NOT ADD ON ALL YOUR MOTHER IN LAW/SISTER-IN-LAW WOES TO HIS LIST OF NEGATIVES.** He's not to be held responsible for everyone's faults.

The same goes for the wife. Alright, so she cribs about the effects of passive smoking and how you're shortening her life by years! You might want to think about it yourself. She's on and on about you not spending enough time with the kids or making enough time for the family. A man has gotta earn, you say. Or maybe it's too close to the truth. So her chicken curry doesn't taste like mama's, but does your mom make pasta like she does? Get the point? You can as much turn your mom into a photocopy of your wife as you can turn your wife into a replica of your mom! God forbid, you say. Then why are you so hung up about these trivial things? You want her to be her own person, believe me. That's why you married her. Appreciate the things she already does well, keeping home, managing the kids and her career if she has one, taking care of your relatives and friends, making peace when the kids fight, getting along with your mother- all this while you still find time for a chilled beer after work. You don't have a monopoly on stress. Take on one complete weekend of managing the home and kids without her help and you'll probably be heading for the nearest anger management course the following weekend.

We don't often see the wood for the trees. Look at the **BIG PICTURE**. Don't nitpick. A good practice is to tell yourself, "Well, at least I don't have to worry about the kids' school work. Or "Thank God he doesn't expect me to be vegan/ vegetarian/ teetotaller conservative, drive mom to hospital/ wedding.... whatever. Stop taking the pluses for granted.

You may be upset, he hasn't taken you to the latest blockbuster movie. So what? Go with your friend/ sister/ colleague/ mom, whoever! Stop whining! Take charge of your own happiness. He hasn't objected, has he? Who's he to stop me you may well ask. But what's to stop him from making a fuss and ruining your day? You may still defy him and go, but would you really be able to make a day of it? You'd probably spend the first half of the movie ranting and raving about the injustice of it all. But then, whoever said life was fair? Not me!

So if you want to savour what you already have, don't take things for granted. Make a conscious effort to appreciate what you have. Yes, I repeat, make a **CONSCIOUS EFFORT.** Take time to notice others' misfortunes – their health issues, financial problems, personal losses, accidents, tragedies, and people who are victims of natural and man-made disasters. People who are victims of physical and emotional abuse and trauma. Now honestly tell me you have nothing to be thankful for or that you're not grossly better off than millions of others. But that doesn't solve my problem, you argue. I still want that groovy car and the snazzy horrendously priced sunglasses.

All in good time, my friend. We're getting there, but there's no need to be miserable all the way to the top. So this is about enjoying your life, your family and your assets while you work your way to the things you actually want, all the time labouring under the assumption that those things would finally guarantee you happiness.

Authentic research by reliable authorities has proved that the happiest country in the world is Finland! Where there is no sunlight for six months of the year. Not the USA, UK or Switzerland, but Finland. I'm not talking about the standard of living or ease of living here. As per 2021 statistics, Finland stands first and USA stands at 16th place in the happiness index. Why would the world's most powerful democracy, the richest, mightiest superpower, the land of opportunity, land of milk and honey not stand first?

What are the parameters? Not money alone. Family values, friends, interpersonal relationships, well-being, physical and mental, achievements and care all go towards measuring the level of happiness.

You and you alone can take charge of your happiness!

HAVE YOU STARTED COUNTING YOUR BLESSINGS YET? TIME IS RUNNING OUT!

Chapter 5

Find the Rose among the Thorns

"Just when the caterpillar thought the world was ending, it turned into a butterfly."

The jackfruit, widely grown in the southern states of India, particularly Kerala and the areas bordering it, parts of Karnataka and Tamil Nadu, is a versatile fruit. In appearance, hardly appetising, even though it grows low, in bunches on the trunk of a sturdy tree. Green, growing to several kilos in weight, it has a thick, thorny outer surface, which when cut open, reveals a mass of pale yellow fibres. Persevere and you will reach the yellow, softer, still fibrous but very sweet kernels inside.

Sweet to taste, rich in nutrients and high in fibre, the fruit can be eaten as such, made into a kheer or a sweet pudding, deep-fried in strips as a savoury snack or made into a curry when still unripe, that tastes much like chicken chunks. Today, it is touted as a vegan substitute and is even made into flour.

If man had not looked beyond the thorny exterior, he might well have missed the sweet fruit within. Much of life passes us by as we fail to grab the opportunities that stare us in the face, much like the jackfruit hanging low on the tree. We hesitate to look past the obvious for we often wonder –

What great benefit could await us beyond such hardships?

Even if we were to persist, who knows if the result would be worth the effort?

We're probably right to a large extent. Maybe even 90% of the time. For what comes to us without effort? Not even a baby is born without nine months of effort from the mother! And yes, maybe the winner of the £1 million sweepstakes!

Would one forgo having children just because one perforce has to go through pregnancy and childbirth? Of course not, you would say. We'll face that when we have to. After all, one can't compare the joy that children bring!

If one were to actually look at a rose garden from afar, as I was doing recently just outside the Public Library in Cubbon Park, Bangalore, one would be astounded by the colour and variety of the roses there. As I went nearer, I saw more of the leaves and thorns than the flowers on each stem. But the eye only enjoys the beauty of the flowers and ignores the unsavoury parts. The brain is the world's fastest and most intelligent supercomputer. It requires nanoseconds to process information. But it has a few aberrations, mostly deliberately configured. For example, one can remember in great detail a tooth extraction or a root canal procedure but try as one might, it's impossible to reproduce the degree of pain one felt at the time. Likewise, one cannot reproduce physical pleasure. But for some reason, it appears that the memory of a pleasurable event lasts longer than that of pain. This is why, mothers never associate their children with the pain of labour, but with the pleasure of their birth. If not, no mother would have a second child.

And no woman, or metrosexual man, for that matter, would have gone back for a waxing session. One only remembers the glamorous result!

So far, I have only touched upon superficial situations. But, for every patient I treat, pain is a very real phenomenon. Peculiarly, since no other individual can perceive someone else's pain at any given time, one has a hypothetical way of assessing its nature and degree. Fortunately or unfortunately, I have been in the position of having to personally experience a great many medical conditions and some very painful and traumatic situations in my own life. Thankfully, though I cannot reproduce the exact severity and nature of the pain, having experienced it has given me immense insight into my patient's condition. It has given me the capacity to empathise with them in a way that would never have been possible otherwise and that no textbook could have taught.

I personally do not regret my ordeal and looking back, a lot of good has come from it. I genuinely look upon those situations as the roses in my life and the thorns have been of little consequence in the larger picture. Though I have to admit, I would have answered differently at the time.

I feel blessed to be able to put myself in my patient's shoes. I find that it gives me a different and deeper perspective on their pain and their anxieties. It makes me strive that much harder to find solutions to their problems in a way that is more than just clinical. The pleasure of having helped someone not merely from a physical ailment, but from an emotional standpoint, is in itself rewarding, certainly beyond the measure of monetary benefit.

That in itself is of great benefit to me personally. It increases my self-worth and boosts my ego and my serotonins no end. I go home happy with myself and my job, transferring that happy feeling to my home and my loved ones. Something like the concept of paying it forward. Obviously, it would directly impact the way they deal with those around them.

Having empathy for others also makes you evaluate your own life and appreciate what you have as opposed to those you're empathising with – things you may have taken completely for granted. For example, the fact that you have children you can dote on, the fact that you have a husband, mother, mother in law or significant other who loves you, that you have no serious health issues etc, most of which are a given, yet things we don't take time to savour.

A great many times, the very things we lament about end up being a boon. Let me tell you about a young friend who met a handsome, intelligent, charming boy, an MBA from a renowned business school, with a great sense of humour and who pursued her relentlessly till she agreed to be his girlfriend. Things worked well for a while and they were constantly on the phone. He soon moved to Europe where his family was and continued to live with his mother and brother while doing his thesis for another masters.

Her life now revolved around the phone and his time zone. She slept at odd hours and woke up at odd hours, rushing home to make calls, leaving little free time for herself. To add to her distress, he was constantly cribbing about his thesis and his mother's debilitating illness. She apparently dint approve of his relationship and made it obvious. The boy went into depression and now all conversation revolved around his mother's illness, her interference and his inability to get done with his thesis. A year and a half later, he was still nowhere near completing his dissertation. He no longer laughed or joked, his visits were few and far between, he was broke and yet she found herself tied down to a relationship that was going nowhere, yet unable to go out with anyone else.

One fine day, he called to say he no longer wanted to be in the relationship. Devastated, she cried for days. All their grand plans of getting married, the house with the picket fence and dog had come to nought. She didn't sleep, eat or smile for days. Her family stood by her, talking and counselling constantly about how she was better off without him and deserved someone better.

Months later, when she got back to work, she realised how stifled she had been in the relationship, constantly trying to live upto his and his family's expectations of her, while foregoing her social life completely, forever listening to his woes and becoming depressed herself. Suddenly, she was her own person, no longer waiting by the phone, able to go out with her friends, do her own thing, and finally able to find her freedom. She started wondering why she had persisted with the relationship in the first place. And she was smiling and laughing again.

We often wear blinds and see only what we want to see. Too often, it is a protective mechanism resorted to in order to prevent ourselves from getting hurt. People sometimes ignore signs of their husband's or boyfriend's infidelity because they are afraid to face the truth. If one were to confront the other person, it could lead to disaster whether it were to be the truth or not. If it turned out to be the truth, it could mean the end of the relationship as we knew it, if not, it would still be devastating to the other person that you lacked trust and change the whole equation of the relationship.

The art of expressing one's fear of insecurity without sounding either confrontational or distrustful is nearly impossible. But sometimes, a clean break is better than a long-standing unhappy or distrustful relationship.

One can be constantly distressed, anxious, depressed or all of these and that could reflect on your physical and mental health, not to mention your work life.

A good option is to write down all the pros and cons of being in the relationship and see which way it tilts. If there are more pluses than minuses, you can still express your love for that person and say how much he/ she means to you. Then bring up the fact that his recent behaviour is making you feel a little unloved and insecure and seek a valid explanation. It could be something as simple as a serious business crisis that has taken up all his concentration, time, money and interest. It could well be one of the reasons he has gone off sex as well. All the things that could make you suspect the worst. And damage your self-esteem.

But if you know the actual cause, it could save you a lot of heartaches. And if the actual cause were to be another woman, well, at least you know where you stand. I agree that finding out one fine day that you're playing second fiddle to someone else could definitely not qualify as the proverbial rose. But it could definitely open up a whole lot of avenues for you... the courage to not put up with what you have been tolerating, the push to do something else with your life that you have been putting on hold...the conviction that you deserve better and the motivation to move out of your rut. If you still feel that the other person deserves a second chance, it is also entirely up to you. You alone are the best judge of what makes you happy.

But that would only happen after the initial phases of denial, anger and acceptance. The initial stage of having the floor cave in has to be dealt with one way or the other. The support of near and dear ones is immeasurable. They could mean the difference between sanity and insanity. But hang in there. Months or years ahead, you will be able to look back at the pain without actually wincing. And you will find the rose, my friend.

BUT LIKE ALL BLOOMS THERE IS A TIME AND A SEASON.

Chapter 6

Acquire a Sense of Humour

"Only two things are infinite, the universe and human stupidity. And I'm not sure about the former."

Albert Einstein.

Life is more than just the sum of its events. It's not maths. More often than not, you will want to tear your hair out. This is why the world's biggest industry is the entertainment industry. The world of movies and make-believe. Music and mayhem. Magic and mystery. Mirth and merriment. Also why actors are paid in millions and doctors in thousands and lakhs. Laughter is the best medicine. And who doesn't like a good laugh? The world of stand-up comedy is an industry by itself. YouTube has dedicated content for comedy scenes from movies. It boasts umpteen subscribers. Why? Because humour is an integral part of our lives. Probably the one thing that differentiates Homo sapiens from other animals. Haven't heard of a dog with a sense of humour have you? Although he might trick you and have the last laugh. Why is a person who can make you laugh considered good company? Simple! Because when he makes you laugh, he manages to increase your happy hormones also known as endorphins. And laughter and happiness are both contagious.

Life often throws strange things at us. We all remember crazy incidents from our younger days when we got into serious trouble, but that we now look back upon with a smile.

Way back in the eighties, while I was studying medicine in what is now called Belagavi, I took a flight home one weekend. Those days there was one single flight to Bangalore that operated three days a week via Goa. I boarded the flight and promptly fell asleep thanks to all the late-night study hours. When I heard the cabin crew announce that we had arrived, I excitedly gathered my things and deplaned. Exiting the hot tarmac and the bright afternoon sun, I entered the arrival building to find a smartly dressed girl in a sari uniform with a brass nameplate pinned to her sari saying "Bogmalo Beach Resort."

Since when did Bangalore get a beach I thought. I was first disoriented and then devastated. The plane was in Goa and I had alighted instead of staying on to proceed to Bangalore. It was meant to transit for just twenty minutes. I panicked, then rushed and met the Indian Airlines staff, went through security check again and managed to get back on the plane finally heaving a sigh of relief.

I find it hilarious today, but it was an agonising twenty minutes.

The ability to laugh at oneself is a wonderful trait and one that will see you through tough times particularly when you find someone else laughing at you. Eleanor Roosevelt once said, "No one can make you feel inferior without your consent." Smile often, it requires fewer muscles than a frown, will prevent wrinkles and crow's feet and get someone else to smile with you.

We're all capable of being annoyed, particularly with our spouses. But look at what Rita Rudner had to say, "I love being married. It's so great to find that one special person you want to annoy for the rest of your life!" Now I have to admit, I have no idea who she was, but she was on to something. There are days when everything's fine. Then again, there are days when I walk around like everything's fine, but deep down, inside my shoe, my sock is slowly sliding off.

Talking of shoes, Covid seems to have put all our footwear to rest. It seems to have taken the fun out of life. Unless you're looking for a seven day room service from your mother in law. Unless, she beats you to it. But hey, at least you get to lock her up for seven days for once in your life.

But seriously, life's not all bad. Bad things happen, but that shouldn't define our lives. You may have lost a job or two, a few lakhs here and there, but hey, you're not in a body bag on the way to going six feet under right? You aren't skydiving with a parachute that won't open right? As Steven Wright said, "If at first you don't succeed, skydiving is definitely not for you."

Life is too short to be taken seriously. So smile while you still have teeth. I don't suggest bumming around. As I said before, have goals and make enough, so losing a couple of lakhs will not kill you. As they say, to succeed in life you need a wishbone, a backbone and a funny bone. Life is hard. No doubt. It was a lot easier when Apple and Blackberry were just fruits. No social media, no Facebook, no Twitter, no Instagram, no peer pressure, likes or unfriending... it wasn't even a word back then. But would you give up any of this? No way, you say. But why give so much power to someone else? Why worry so much about someone else's opinion of what you eat, wear, drink, talk... whatever? Be self-confident. Be silly. Do the things that make you laugh, and be with people who make you laugh. Better yet, make them laugh. I actually love doing that except for a minor detail. I forget the punchline. But what the heck? That makes them laugh even more.

Chapter 7

Turn Around Your Losses
Ctrl + Alt + Del

"If you're going through hell, keep going."

Winston Churchill

For those of you who are unfamiliar, on a PC or laptop with a Windows operating system, Ctrl Alt Del is the combination of keys that a user can press at the same time to terminate an application task or to reboot the operating system.

It also brings up the Task Manager window or a drop-down menu that allows a user to see the status of all currently running programs and to terminate any of them. One can also close a frozen application or shut down or restart the computer.

Does this ring a bell? The human brain is one of the oldest, fastest and most advanced computers known to man. As a doctor privy to the workings of the human body, I can vouch for it. The span of its functions is mind-boggling. And yet, sometimes, we're frozen on the same programs without knowing which keys to press. Life is a series of windows, often overlapping each other, much like the programs on our laptops. Sometimes, we choose to close some of them, but more often than not, we have multiple windows all open at the same time. And then it hangs. We're frozen, not knowing how to proceed, too afraid to close any window, for fear that we may permanently close our options. But at times, we need to press the Ctrl Alt Del keys in our lives, close a program and reboot.

Let me give you an example. When I decided that it was time to slow down slightly at least in terms of my commute, I decided to move my evening clinic closer home. I had been eyeing a potential clinic in a building that was walking distance from home. The location was perfect, it had a nice glass facade, was on the corner of the first floor and had great visibility. The perfect corner office. Even though it was not yet complete, I negotiated with the landlord and over several meetings finalised the deal. Excited, I called my architect and interior designer and my dear friend planned the layout, the furniture, the colour scheme, the reception and waiting area and in no time had the furniture made. Closer to completion there were differences with the owner over the rent and other additional charges. Disappointed, I had a discussion with my family and decided it wouldn't work out. I had already spent a huge sum of money on the furniture, printer, instruments and whatnot. But with a heavy heart, I gave up the idea. It was the best decision I could have made. Six months later Covid hit and I know it would have hit my practice badly as I was new to the area. I saved thousands each month on rent, salaries and recurring expenditure even though my furniture languished in the basement. I slowly picked up practice by starting a clinic at my home where I had already made provision for practice. I didn't need to pay rent and I didn't need to commute. I even managed to get rid of the extra furniture after retaining what I needed.

Often, one needs to have the courage to close a few windows, open a few new ones and be able to reboot. Have faith in the adage that when God closes one door, he opens a window. Easier said than done.

Sometimes a rut may seem like the more comfortable option. Ask any woman who is facing domestic abuse and she will tell you that the thought of leaving is scarier than staying. The incidence of domestic abuse went up drastically during the Covid lockdown. With husbands working from home, women had no respite. With themselves working from home, they had nowhere to run and nowhere to hide even for those eight working hours. I'm not talking of third-world countries here if that's what you're thinking. The rates went up alarmingly in countries like France, Spain and the US. But empowerment is not gender-baised. A man could equally be at the receiving end of domestic abuse and mental cruelty. It is each individual who needs to have a Ctrl Alt Del option that starts in the mind.

We are all victims of situations that may not necessarily be of our own making. But we definitely should have the courage to say "No," loudly, strongly and with conviction. To learn to bury the past and move on, to have faith in another monsoon after a drought and to explore all options. If you're already in a pit, the only way out is up.

The thing about smart people is that they seem like crazy people to dumb people. So someone said. And it couldn't be more true. So regardless of what others think of you, cut your losses and do what's best for you. If you don't look out for yourself, no one will.

"I have not failed. I've just found 10000 ways that won't work."

Thomas. A. Edison

RIDING ALONG THE SAME RUT ONLY MAKES IT DEEPER.

Chapter 8

Look Cheerful - Be Compassionate.

"Don't confuse my personality with my attitude. My personality is who I am, my attitude depends on who you are."

Being cheerful is an art. Looking cheerful is an even bigger art. Practice it long enough and it will soon become a part of your persona.

Take the example of doctors. I have had days when my maid has quit suddenly, I've had to leave urgently for a delivery admission without breakfast, there was no lunch to go home to, the house hadn't been cleaned, my slipper sole had come apart (yes, I keep a spare in the boot of my car) and yet I have gone on my ward rounds cheerfully pepping up my patients, delivering another patient and celebrating with the family. It's called boxing. Not the Mary Kom / Mike Tyson kind - the one where you punch your opponent senseless. It's the one where you compartmentalise and box your events, situations etc into separate boxes in your head.

I leave the home, maid, and lunch in a different box and come to work. I still have the capacity to think clinically, plan my day, order food and cheer up my patient with infertility or even a mother-in-law problem. Once she is sorted, I'm not just trying to look cheerful, I'm feeling cheerful, happy for her and happy for me that I could sort it out.

Someone once said, "Make sure the enemy doesn't lie between your ears!" We are solely responsible for maximising or minimising our problems. The trick is to think beyond the problem to the solution. A diamond is merely a lump of coal that did well under pressure. But I'm hoping you won't need that long!

Every so often, just when a doctor is all set to leave to the movies, an emergency lands up. There are those who have started to leave town and have had to come back for a patient. Can't very well pounce on the patient, can you? One not only has to look cheerful, one has to be reassuring, get down to work and then think of the backlash from the kids. No mean task. I'm very sure such crises crop up all the time regardless of which field you're working in. One has to learn to adapt, think on your feet and think out of the box. But over time it becomes a habit, one that has to be cultivated carefully and sincerely. Often it's our demeanour that makes people love us or look up to us. As I said before, the more you give, the more you get. Your emotional quotient can determine the difference between success and failure. And patience is what you have when there are too many witnesses.

You might say, you're talking about small problems. What about major stuff? Like what? A break up? Divorce? Job loss? Illness? How does one stay cheerful?

I get it. But clichéd as it sounds, what doesn't kill you makes you stronger. If you had a breakup, it was for a reason. One doesn't break up with someone as a pastime. Obviously, there were incompatibilities that could not be sorted. Or, either one of you was not so into the relationship. Or the families weren't and you don't have the guts, the money or the wherewithal to go your own way. Or you're used to being funded by Pops. Whatever!

Obviously, one of you has decided it's not workable. And it takes two to tango. Or you're fed up of one another's traits and decided you cannot live with them lifelong. Fair enough. It's not a crime. So why the guilt trip? Because you want to eat the cake and have it too! And if you're the one who was dumped, well, he or she doesn't deserve you anyway. And maybe they're right. Perhaps you're not really as suited to each other as you thought. It's not a crime. There are more suitable fish in the sea. Suitable for you and suitable for him or her as well.

Having said that, I'm not denying that it can be devastating. Time heals all wounds. Que sera sera. When you bump into that person twenty years down the line, you will probably look at your husband or wife and two beautiful kids and thank your stars.

Are you one of those people who like cold wars? The kind that go on for days, if not weeks! The kind where you don't make eye contact, answer in monosyllables and bang utensils while mumbling under your breath?

Look what the Cold War did to US and Russia decades ago! It got a lot of James Bond movies made for sure. It also financed a lot of double agents I might add. In fact, you might be encouraging a few of those yourself...maids, siblings, neighbours, friends, who are privy to your fights and will be dying to tell you what the other person said.

Take it from me, not much good will come of it. Apart from not resolving the issue, it will internalise your anxiety and lead to hypertension, stress, insomnia, bad temper, gastritis, depression and unproductivity at work. Without of course solving the original problem. Silence speaks volumes I agree. But it can also be deafening. It can widen the distance so much that it can make you feel like you're world's apart, physically, mentally and emotionally. This can happen not only with spouses, lovers or friends, it can happen with siblings, parents or colleagues.

Sadly, the issue that triggers it is often trivial, most often monetory or material. In the larger scheme of things, it's really not worth it. The Bhagvad Gita prescribes the notion of attachment with detachment. Ultimately, nothing is really ours, except the emotions we show. Any situation, within reason, can be diffused by making light of it or sleeping over it and rethinking.

At least give it a shot. Honestly. Someone angry with you Smile and say sorry. How long can they be upset with you? Give a hug and mom will melt for sure. Harsh words cannot be undone and fester like a wound that doesn't heal.

Take to the habit of mirroring. We often consciously or unconsciously mirror what the other person does or says. If they are always polite and sweet we mirror them. If someone is respectful, we're respectful too. But if they are rude, we are rude back. But if we develop the art of being nice, the other person begins to mirror us. It's that easy. And who can resist being cheerful when you embody sweetness and good cheer?

Compassion is a different ballgame. Not everyone is capable of compassion. There are some people who are in the spectrum, the Autistic Spectrum. They naturally have a low EQ and can be highly misunderstood. This can make them even more wary, introverted and aloof. One can only be patient and understanding if one is aware. They're often labelled as being snobbish or superior. And more often than not they are brilliant. Or they could be insecure. Before you judge someone, walk a mile in their shoes. After that, who cares? You're a mile away from them and you've got their shoes! But on a serious note, acquire the habit of being non-judgemental. Again, it is a conscious and learnt habit. We have no idea what the other person's journey has been.

I recently adopted a dog off the street. He was a handsome fella, half Alsatian, about two years old, randomly running in and out of houses with a searching look. I never heard him bark. By and by, he started spending more time at our place and we started feeding him regularly. Initially, he just came during the day. Soon he stayed the night as well. It's a no strings attached relationship, I joked with my daughter. She laughed. "We'll see", she said. He hadn't yet made a sound. He didn't make eye contact. I assumed he had been traumatised. After a month, he made small noises, when the glass patio door was closed. Before long, he staked his place and began to bark at any stranger who so much as dared to enter the gate. He had found his space. And his home. I called the vet, got him dewormed, vaccinated and checked, bought a collar, ordered a bed and called him Sunny. My daughter just smiled. He jumps for joy every time I come back home and can't get enough of getting his head patted and massaged. He's now the love of my life. The one with a bark bigger than mine!

I REST MY CASE.

Chapter 9

Find Your Passion - You'll Never Know Boredom

"Learn to balance a dream and a job until your dream becomes your job."

Are you one of those people who wake up every morning thinking, "Oh no, not another day of the same old, same old!"

No prizes for guessing then that what you're doing is not what you're passionate about. No matter. Not everyone gets their dream job or any job at all!

My dream job might have been to get paid to travel the world, meet different people, taste different foods, experience different cultures and have my own show on television without spending a dime. But hey, I'm equally happy doing what I do and I love it.

If your job is not your passion, find one. It may be painting a planter box or planting a tree, baking cookies or baking brownies, doing watercolours or knitting a winter coat. A passion is something that you're willing to do even if it tires you out or one that will not tire you out however long you're at it. Would you go out of your way to get the girl or man of your dreams? Put your heart and soul trying to woo her? Lose sleep over her? And yet be excited at the thought of another day, another chance, another word, text or glance? That's what passion is about. A certain dedication to your cause, whatever it may be. The kind that makes you cook your kids' favourite dish or dress your little doll in a fancy dress for the competition. Passion gives meaning to life. The incentive to achieve, the drive to succeed while making the journey worthwhile. It's the fuel that runs the car heading towards its destination.

If you don't have a passion, find one. And I don't mean the other woman! Often, our jobs are just a means to put food on the table and take care of our finances. But there is always a dream at the back of our minds. Rekindle that dream. Mine was to write.

Perhaps it was a game you loved in your childhood... badminton or tennis or cricket. Maybe you want to find something new. Golf perhaps? Crochet? Mehendi? Charcoal painting? There's always YouTube to push you along. One doesn't know till one has tried. Lockdown discovered thousands of closet chefs. Give yourself a purpose. The mundane will always be there. There's no escaping our daily chores. Ignite that spark. Step on it! Take the plunge! There's nothing to lose. All you will find is the motivation to do something that will make you happy. And you will never feel alone in your own company ever again.

GRAB THOSE TENNIS SHOES, THAT PAINT BRUSH, THAT COOKIE CUTTER...
AND YES... GO GET YOUR GIRL! NOW!!

Chapter 10

Mind Over Matter

"Old age comes at a bad time. Just when you finally know everything, you start to forget everything you know."

You are as young as you feel. So they say. But not everyone is blessed with good health. And it's extremely tough to be happy and cheerful when one is suffering from ill health, be it osteoarthritis or angina, colitis or Corona, myalgia or migraine. But sitting there moaning will not cut it. One has to learn to accept the condition in the first place and find a solution. Whether that is allopathy or alternative medicine is a personal choice. But making sure you take charge and treat it is half the battle.

But sadly, medication alone will not often cure it. A positive attitude, the conviction that it will get better, faith in your physician and the desire to get better are all equally important.

Research has shown that faith and prayer actually increase your T cell counts and improve immunity. In a study of cardiac patients who underwent angioplasty, one-half of the patients who religiously prayed every day showed more angiogenesis or more new blood vessel formation than those who did not pray. As a surgeon, I have found that patients who are cheerful, positive and with complete faith in their treating physician or surgeon have better outcomes, while those who are always in doubt about the results invariably are among those with complications.

In a study conducted by Harvard Medical School, researchers found that relaxation techniques including repetitive prayer and mantra activated 'disease fighting genes' and improved immunity.

In an article by Luke Cutinho, published in 2020, he explains the miracle of prayer. He tells us that everything is energy, the food we eat, the water we drink, the air we breathe. We ourselves are nothing but a form of energy. We create good or bad energy. Prayer done sincerely can convert bad energy to good energy.

How do they affect us at the genetic level? He explains that prayers awaken certain emotions that have the ability to turn on or off certain genes. While healthy lifestyles turn on genes that can repair and heal you, unhealthy lifestyles turn on genes that lead to sickness and disease. This is called epigenetics where 'epi' stands for environment and its ability to control certain genes. Apparently watching a funny movie with friends can turn on 700 genes related to our immune system. But an anxious, angry lifestyle can also turn off these same 700 genes, lowering your immunity.

Cha et all studied 219 consecutive infertile women aged 24 to 29 years who were treated with IVF and embryo transfer in Seoul, Korea. They were randomised into distant prayer and control groups. Prayer groups conducted prayers in USA, Canada and Australia. The patients, providers, investigators and statisticians did not know about prayer allocations. Therefore, it was triple blind.

Cha et al found that women who had been prayed for had nearly twice the pregnancy rate as the other group and also showed a higher implantation rate. Benefits were independent of clinical or laboratory providers.

Prayer and meditation have also been known to decrease anxiety, stress, high blood pressure and cortisol levels as well as depression.

No doubt some conditions are chronic, debilitating, painful and resistant to treatment. Be the best you can and do the best you can. It will save you and the people around you from getting depressed.

At eighty-nine, my mother had severe lower limb ischemia, a non-healing ulcer on her foot, a pacemaker and was in congestive heart failure. A Gynaecologist herself, she took her medications regularly and troubled no one, though she was breathless even walking to the restroom and back. She had written a DNR – DO NOT RESUSCITATE - clause and wished to die at home.
One day she said, “Neither of them is going!”
“Who?” I asked.
“Neither breathlessness nor life!

They're both fighting and saying, 'I'm not going! I'm not going!' And to top it all, this wound on my foot, hanging on like a pet dog!"
I laughed.

"Ma, you're crazy!" I said.
She was. With an amazing sense of humour and cheerful till her last day, she personified elegance, grace and positivity.

Sheer willpower can overcome adversity. It's easy to lapse into depression. In fact, depression is so rampant worldwide, it has reached epidemic proportions. It is a mental health disorder that affects how a person feels, thinks and acts.

While Ukraine and the USA have the highest rates of depression as per 2022 statistics, underdeveloped countries may not have documented cases and therefore scores of cases go undetected.
Depression is characterised by:

- A persistent feeling of sadness
- Loss of interest in activities once enjoyed
- Change in appetite, loss or gain in weight
- Trouble in sleeping
- Fatigue or loss of energy
- Slow movements or speech
- Loss of memory
- Lack of self-confidence
- The feeling of guilt or worthlessness

- Difficulty in concentration at school or work
- Being short-tempered
- Low sexual drive
- Suicidal thoughts

Any or all of these symptoms need to be addressed either in person or by those around them. Timely help could avert serious consequences. It has always been taboo to admit to a mental health disorder. But the scenario is slowly changing. Unlike in the West, therapy has always been considered the last straw. With nuclear families, interpersonal relationships have changed. People feel isolated, no longer having access to households with a large number of family members where one could confide in a brother, sister, cousin or aunt, and lighten the burden of a situation without the problem exiting the walls of the house.

With Metaverse, where you can actually buy clothes, property or cars in the virtual world, the whole equation of relationships whether it is with things or people has changed dramatically. Technically, one might own a mansion on Metaverse, but what happens when you come home to your tiny, messy apartment in Mumbai or London? Who has to clean up? Is it escapism or vicarious living? Will it make us less inclusive and less dependent on interpersonal relationships in the real world?

Technically, the concept of the Metaverse is not new to Hindu philosophy. It subscribed to the concept of

'Maya'. It believed that the whole universal experience is an illusion and we live in a matrix. That is a hard concept for the common man to digest. Manu Bhaumik, in his book, 'Code name God' has tried to amalgamate science and the Universal Consciousness, or God as we like to call Him. Notwithstanding the quantum physics, we will still have a dirty house to come back to in the world as we know it.

Today, though one has five hundred friends on Facebook, umpteen followers, hundreds of likes and heaps of praises on WhatsApp, one feels a constant pressure to keep up or outdo the Joneses. There is a continuous need for approval and validation from friends to strangers. Even the lack of response from an expected source could cause anxiety.

I have come across scores of patients with infertility issues where the problem is not a serious medical one, but merely a lack of desire to have sex with the spouse. Watching porn is one of the major factors for this lack of intimacy. Likewise, social media interactions could sabotage personal relationships.

With a generation that is increasingly self-obsessed and self-centred, hundreds of friends on social media platforms may not translate into even a few genuine friends in real life. . The kind who will have your back, come what may. It's important to make true friends and have a strong bond with those around us. Friends are the family you weren't born with. This can largely prevent depression and offset the trauma, physical or mental, of any medical condition one is suffering from.

Speaking of new-age maladies, I recently happened to attend a conference where the topic of discussion was, **"ENDOCRINE DISRUPTORS"**. It referred to all those factors that played havoc with our hormones including pesticides in food and water, contamination with Nano particles from plastic waste that enters our fruits and vegetables from the soil, microwaves, Teflon-coated cookware, preservatives in processed food, lead poisoning from emissions and heating food in plastic containers. They lead to thyroid disorders, polycystic ovaries, anovulation and lower sperm counts, as well as a host of other problems.

Sustainable living practices like our age-old practice of heating food in steel vessels, cooking in earthen pots and cast iron woks, storing water in copper vessels, cooking in ghee as opposed to hydrogenated vegetable oils and discarding the habit of using disposable plastic and paper cups can go a long way in ensuring a better life. The practice of eating on banana leaves and carrying food in containers made of leaves stitched together to make bowls called '**donnes**' had much going for it. Eating on banana leaves helps the food absorb the polyphenols in it, which are natural antioxidants also found in green tea. They battle the free radicals in the body and help prevent diseases. Banana leaves are also said to have anti-bacterial properties. Sustainable living practices go a long way in maintaining a healthy body and mind. But that is a whole topic in itself.

Ultimately, it's the mind that wins over the body. It is as important to want to stay healthy as it is to stay healthy. Having said that, it's just as important to have your own back. Make a concrete plan to invest in insurance to take care of your health without having to depend on anyone, even your own children. Make provision for emergencies. Knowing that your health or other concerns can be taken care of, can in itself give a sense of relief and well-being.

Have your life sorted, be positive and cheerful and happiness will no longer be what you're looking for. It will become a state of being. . Every new day is another chance to change your life for the better. It's your mind that needs convincing. Have a game plan. and make up your mind to **REBOOT, REINVENT, RECHARGE.**

Carpé Diem! As the Italians would say! Seize the day!
Cheers!

About The Author

Dr. Chitra Reddy is a practising Obstetrician, Gynaecologist, IVF & Infertility Specialist with over three decades of experience in the field. Her wide experience in dealing with people from all walks of life has resulted in her gathering some simple nuggets of wisdom on finding the path to happiness, living a life less complicated, and finding contentment in everyday life. She has published a book of poems, "Nuances", dealing with varied subjects, from love to envy, success to despair. She is an avid traveller, loves to cook, bake, paint in oils and play golf when time permits. She lives in Bangalore, India.

GRAB A COPY

On Amazon

Nuances' is the assimilation of the essence of life as the author knows it, ever since she started penning poetry at the age of thirteen. Life as a medical student, an intern, a wife, a mother, a surgeon, an infertility specialist as well as the day to day events around her have shaped her thoughts in this collection of poems which bring out the subtle nuances that colour the world around us.

Notes

Notes

Keep Connected

Instagram- @chitra.reddy.526
Email- chitraramanreddy@gmail.com
Website – www.drchitrareddy.com